THE
EMAIL
COMMUNICATION
BIBLE

WRITE BETTER EMAILS AT WORK

- 18 Time-Saving Templates
- 10 Helpful A.I. Prompts

AMY LANCI

Print ISBN: 979-8-9905482-0-6
Ebook ISBN: 979-8-9905482-1-3

Library of Congress Control Number: 2024908652

Printed in the United States

Dedicated to the people in my life who helped me to believe in my voice.

Contents

Introduction

The inspiration that sparked this book was born several decades ago, when my grandparents were two teenagers, who lived in a little village in Guangzhou, China.

Shortly after getting married, my grandfather went to the United States to help his father and his brother to build their family business while my grandmother stayed behind in China to help her mother-in-law.

Because this was the time before emails, texts, smartphones, and computers, the only way my grandparents could stay in touch was by writing old-fashioned letters and sending them through the global postal system. Sending those letters took weeks, sometimes months. Could you imagine how the wait felt to my grandparents? Long, for sure! Nevertheless, this was how they kept their love and connection alive the entire time they were apart.

After 13 long years, they were finally reunited and were together for the rest of their lives.

So much has changed since my grandparents' time. We have a much greater ability to communicate with people from around the world in real-time through video chat, text, phone calls and of course, email. Communication is more accessible than ever! And yet, finding connection (like the kind my grandparents had) is still something we have to actively seek out, like buried treasure. To build trust with someone in your personal and professional relationships, you have to be willing to invest the time and energy to get to know them and let them know who you are. That's why the saying, "you have to walk a mile in someone else's shoes" exists. One mile is not a huge distance, but it is long enough to require a good amount of time and energy.

When you think about building a repertoire with your boss, your coworkers, or your clients, you have the chance to walk many miles, in all of their shoes. A closet-full perhaps! To be able to see their point-of-view and pay close attention to their requests and questions, you have an opportunity to show your professionalism, encourage healthy teamwork, meet your project goals, and grow in your career, while also minimizing your involvement in sticky situations.

That's the real power of connection. When you are able to really speak the language of your recipient, you are able to work better and smarter together, in a more peaceful way. And it all starts with your inbox.

Use this email communication bible to get to know your boss, your coworkers, and your clients on a deeper level. Take into account how they are processing information in their individual roles, and what they really need from you in order to complete their projects and help you with your questions. By implementing the strategies in this book, you may be surprised to see how the world around you changes. Once you master the art of email communication, you will start to see a glimmer of what my grandparents had.

Start Here

If you're feeling like your words are getting lost in translation when it comes to your emails, you're not wrong.

In the Digital Age, it is easier and faster to get in touch with somebody without ever speaking with them face-to-face or voice-to-voice. Email, text, messenger platforms and social media have allowed us to reach out and stay-in-touch with people from all over the world at the push of a button. You can send an email to someone half-way across the world and know it will get there in a matter of seconds. No need for snail mail or sending smoke signals!

While we've gained a lot from the Digital Age, we've lost a lot too and that's where the *real* problem lies.

If you're sitting in a room with someone, think about all the things you notice about them:

- The tone of their voice
- Their body language
- Their facial expressions
- Their physical reactions to different topics and words
- Their attention to their physical appearance
- The energy they carry

All of these are vital cues and clues that are readily available anytime you meet someone in-person, whether it is someone new or someone you have known for a long time.

Now, let's take the same list and see what cues you are left with when it comes to speaking to someone on the phone.

- The tone of their voice
- ~~Their body language~~
- ~~Their facial expressions~~
- ~~Their physical reactions to different topics and words~~
- ~~Their attention to their physical appearance~~
- The energy they carry

Notice that we are now left with only 2 out of the 6 cues, which means we have 67% less to work with!

Finally, let's look at email. This is what we're left with:

- The tone of their voice
- ~~Their body language~~
- ~~Their facial expressions~~
- ~~Their physical reactions to different topics and words~~
- ~~Their attention to their physical appearance~~
- ~~The energy they carry~~

Now, we're down to only the tone of voice. Even then, you can only receive this *indirectly* because you're hearing it through your recipient's word choices, not by the sound of their voice.

Taking all of this into account, it's no wonder it is easy to have poor communication through your inbox!

So then…what does that leave you with? How do you bridge the virtual communication gap when your career and job heavily depends on speaking to people through email?

Have no fear, that's why you're here! As a business owner and as someone who has worked within and consulted organizations and teams of different sizes, I have learned the in's and out's of email communication through application, my observations, and what I tested.

In the following chapters, you will learn what you need to know about email communication so you can get projects done in a smooth and timely manner with your coworkers, stay on your boss's good side, and nurture your professional relationships with your clients. Throughout this book, you discover how to anticipate what your email recipient needs to hear from you and how to word your message in just the right way to minimize drama and reach solutions faster.

Bridging The Email Gap

When you are unable to use cues that would normally be available when meeting someone in-person or speaking with them on the phone, what *can* you rely on to help you communicate effectively to your boss, your coworkers and your customers through email? How can you make sure you cover all of your bases when answering questions and troubleshooting issues, without making a bigger mess?

You rely on other skills and talents, that's how! These include empathy, emotional intelligence, critical thinking and a strategy-based approach.

Here's how each of these elements contributes to crafting effective email communication:

1. **Empathy**: Understanding and empathizing with your recipient's perspective, emotions, and needs is crucial for tailoring your communication appropriately. For instance, you can ask yourself, "Is my coworker/boss super busy and feeling overwhelmed?" If the answer is "yes", you will need to figure out the right tone and words to acknowledge their time is limited and your intention is to not add more to their plate. Empathy helps you anticipate how your message will be received and allows you to adjust your tone and content accordingly. When you practice seeing yourself through your

recipient's eyes, you are able to see their perspective and get a clearer idea on what they need to hear for the conversation to go well.

2. **Emotional Intelligence**: Emotional intelligence enables you to manage your own emotions and understand those of others. It helps you choose the right words and tone to convey your message effectively while considering the emotional impact on the recipient. Being emotionally intelligent allows you to navigate potential conflicts, maintain professionalism, and build positive relationships through your email communication. For example, if you are having a less-than-ideal day, you may risk getting frustrated with your team member through email without meaning to. The more aware you are of your needs, the more that will be reflected in your email communication.

3. **Critical Thinking**: Critical thinking involves analyzing information, evaluating its relevance and accuracy, and making conclusions based on objectivity. Practicing critical thinking allows you to assess the purpose and significance of your message, determine the most effective way to convey it, and anticipate potential implications or consequences. In other words, critical thinking reminds you to ask yourself *why* you are writing the email and *what* you will need to say, after processing *how* your recipient will react . This method is so important to identify any blind spots you may have

and anticipate any questions that your recipient may want to ask you.

4. **Strategy**: Strategic thinking involves planning and executing actions to achieve specific goals or objectives. With strategic thinking, you can figure out the underlying purpose or objective of your message, consider the broader context and implications, and develop a plan to achieve your desired outcome. It involves considering factors such as timing, audience, tone, and content to ensure your email aligns with your overarching communication strategy. With every email, you will need to have a clear understanding of what you would like to happen as a result and then consider what you need to write in order to get to that result. Think about *what* you want to accomplish by writing your email and then work backwards to figure out what words will help you get there.

Now, let's explore how each of these elements work together when applied to your emails in a professional setting:

- **Tone**: Empathy and emotional intelligence help you gauge the recipient's emotional state and preferences, allowing you to choose an appropriate tone that resonates with them and fosters positive engagement.

- **Messaging**: Critical thinking and strategic thinking enable you to craft a clear and compelling message that effectively conveys your intended meaning while considering the recipient's perspective and communication style.

- **The "why" behind the email**: Critical thinking helps you identify the underlying purpose or objective of your email, while empathy allows you to consider how your message will impact the recipient and why it matters to them.

- **Background information or context**: Empathy and critical thinking help you anticipate the recipient's knowledge and understanding of the topic, allowing you to provide necessary background information or context to ensure clarity and comprehension.

- **Your relationship with the recipient**: Empathy and emotional intelligence help you navigate the dynamics of your relationship with the recipient, allowing you to tailor your communication to their preferences, level of familiarity, and communication style.

- **Roles, agreements, and boundaries**: Strategic thinking enables you to consider the broader organizational context, including roles, responsibilities, and boundaries, when crafting your email. It helps you communicate in a manner that respects relevant agreements, protocols, and professional norms.

By utilizing empathy, emotional intelligence, critical thinking, and a strategic approach in your email communication like building blocks, you will have an easier time conveying what you need to say to the right audience, in the way you wish to be received.

Your Voice Has Power

Anytime you communicate with customers, coworkers and your boss while you're clocked in, you are speaking as a representative of the company. Every word you speak, whether written or spoken, gives a little sample of the company's brand and culture to everyone you come across. That's why it is crucial for you, as a team member, to be aligned with the company's brand values, voice, and mission.

Matching up the right words with your company's values is important for the following reasons:

1. **Consistency**: Consistently reinforcing the company's identity and builds trust with your customers, because that's the experience they signed up for. Your company's customers expect to have a unique journey while working with you, and if you are using language that is inconsistent with your company's voice, then the customers may feel like they did not get what they paid for. When you embody the brand values, voice, and mission in their email communication, you create a cohesive and unified experience for your customers, as well as your fellow team members and supervisors.

2. **Brand Reputation**: Every email sent by you is an opportunity to shape the company's brand perception. Consistent adherence to the company's brand values

and voice helps reinforce a positive brand image and reputation in the minds of recipients. Conversely, inconsistent or off-brand communication may confuse or undermine the company's brand identity, leading to potential reputational damage. For example, if your company is known for being nurturing and encouraging, you wouldn't respond to a customer with tough love and leave them to figure out a tough issue on their own. Instead, you would use words to show kindness and immediately direct them to people who could help them if you didn't know the answer to their question.

3. **Clarity and Understanding**: Aligning with the company's mission and values will help you to communicate with clarity and purpose. When emails reflect the company's overarching goals and values, recipients, including customers, coworkers, and supervisors, are more likely to understand the context and significance of the message, which fosters meaningful connections with stakeholders and everyone else at your company. You can do this by bringing up examples from your company's most well-known case studies and success stories and relating them to the topic of your discussion in a way that makes sense. For example, if you are giving feedback to your team member to help them improve their sales skills, you can bring up how the founder of your company had to do the same by knocking on 20 doors a day before they started selling products and services like hotcakes!

4. **Relationship Building**: Effective email communication is essential for building and maintaining relationships with everyone you speak to, within the company and outside of it. When you are clear on the company's values and principles, you are able to talk about or demonstrate them in a way that is organic and natural with whomever you are speaking to. If you are helping a client with a technical issue, and your company's top values are honesty and encouragement, you will need to find a way to get to the root of the real issue, explain it plain and simple for your customer, and then let them know you will work with them to figure it out.

5. **Professionalism**: Adhering to the company's brand values and voice in email communication demonstrates professionalism and dedication to representing the organization in the best light. It reflects a sense of pride and ownership in the company's mission and values, showing everyone how well you can uphold the company's standards of excellence in all interactions. If your company prides itself on delivering speedy and high-quality service, then you will need to make sure you respond to your inquiries in a timely manner and give updates when an issue is taking longer than expected, without getting prompted by your recipient, who is waiting to hear back from you.

Overall, being aligned with the company's brand values, voice, and mission when communicating via email is essential for maintaining consistency, enhancing brand reputation, adopting clarity and understanding, building relationships, and demonstrating professionalism. By embodying the company's identity and principles in your written communication, you are able to contribute to the overall success and reputation of the organization. When your voice is consistent in written and spoken communication, you are able to create the experience your customers paid for.

The Run to Inbox Zero

Do you have hundreds of unread and unsorted emails?

Are you getting dozens of messages each day, and you're checking and answering them frequently?

Do you sometimes frantically search through your archives, because you're looking for an important piece of information that can only be found in ONE buried email?

If you said "yes" to any of the above, your inbox is impacting your workflow.

Believe it or not, you have an emotional relationship with your inbox. It's the hub for communication with everyone you work with. If it is constantly overfilled with messages, you risk requests falling through the cracks or hindering your ability to recover information when you need it most. The more these problems persist, the more they will impact your ability to communicate calmly and clearly through your emails.

Think about it. If you're trying to answer 20 to 30 emails a day, you may be tempted to get through your messages as quickly as you can and possibly miss some important details. Even your replies may be impacted, writing short sentences to explain a complex issue as opposed to writing out full paragraphs to give background context. All of this is a recipe for potential sticky situations in the future.

On the other hand, when your emails are well organized and you have an effective strategy for prioritizing which emails need your attention first, you will be able to keep track of your emails in a much calmer fashion and be in a better position to address issues that need your attention.

Therefore, dealing with your email clutter will drastically help with your email communication.

That's why I recommend that you aim to get rid of all the emails in your inbox at the end of every day, otherwise known as "inbox zero." To achieve inbox zero you will need to make sure that the most critical emails are addressed and dealt with and file away the other emails that can wait another day or two for a response. The point of inbox zero is to make a daily habit to keep your emails at bay, so nothing falls through the cracks and you can have peace of mind.

To reach inbox zero, you will need to need to address the following:

Decide on how quickly you need to respond

Just because an email makes its way to your inbox, doesn't mean you need to respond to it as quickly as possible. This doesn't mean you have permission to slack off or not answer emails. In fact, this is the opposite of that. By deciding how quickly to respond, you are actively evaluating how urgent an issue is and whether or not it needs your attention now, or tomorrow.

Plus, when you make it a habit to answer all of your emails quickly, you are setting a precedent with your coworkers and your boss that you will respond at that same pace, no matter what. This is an unrealistic expectation. When you take the time to figure out when you plan to respond to an email, you slowly reset this expectation to a standard that will be more productive and helpful to you.

Here is how you can get started: Whenever you receive an email, read it over and think to yourself, "Does this need to be answered now, or can it wait until tomorrow?" If it is clear this matter needs a response now, take the time to write a reply. If it looks like you can wait until the next day, then snooze the email or put it away in another folder marked as "tomorrow."

Decide how you want to use your inbox

It's clear that email is a means to communicate with your clients and your team virtually, but are you also using your inbox as a file storage system? Or as a task manager? If you are set on clearing away the email clutter, you have to be willing to rethink how you want to use your inbox.

If you do not want to continue searching for important information in your email, you will need to make sure to save the information on your computer or a cloud drive.

Should you want to take more control over what tasks you do during the day, you will need to keep track of your tasks and projects on a separate spreadsheet or project management system to keep everything in front of you. Keeping tasks as unread emails in your email client or putting them in your normal calendar may make it hard to keep track of tasks, especially if you are unable to get to them during the time assigned.

While all of these suggestions will require some time to set up and implement, once they are running at full speed, your inbox will be so much more manageable.

Decide how you want to respond to each email

Since this is a book about email communication, this goes without saying. Whether you choose to pursue inbox zero or you just want to do a better job of organizing your messages, you will always need to thoroughly read over each and every email you receive and think about your response before you start writing. You don't want to risk misreading an email from your boss or your coworkers and then sending a response that creates further confusion and more time delays. No matter how busy things get at work, always make sure you fully understand an email before responding!

The next time you look at your inbox and count how many emails you get in a given day, think about how this is impacting your workflow and thought processes around your tasks and your projects. If you discover that your email has become one of your greatest stressors, consider any of the strategies in this section to help you get organized and get back in control!

9 Signs You Need To Go From Email To Phone

Technology has come a long way, but it is still not perfect. While email offers convenience and a written record of communication, certain situations require the immediate attention, clarity, and nuance that only a phone conversation can provide.

If your email conversation shows at least one of these 9 signs, you will be best served to speak to your recipient over the phone instead:

1. Complex or Sensitive Topics:

Some topics are too complex or sensitive to be effectively communicated through email alone. Delicate matters such as performance evaluations, disciplinary actions, or personal issues are best discussed over the phone to protect yours or your team member's privacy and can be answered with patience and care. This way, you have less back-and-forth and can have a heart-to-heart to discuss these kinds of matters.

2. Urgent or Time-Sensitive Matters:

When time is of the essence, waiting for an email response may not be realistic. Urgent matters requiring immediate attention, such as project deadlines, emergencies, or last-minute changes, warrant a quick phone call to nip issues in the bud right away. Situations that require quick decision-making also warrants a phone call. Whether you are resolving a crisis, coordinating an urgent task, or confirming important details, picking up the phone will ensure you will get the help you need in the nick of time.

3. Misunderstandings or Confusion:

Email communication can sometimes lead to misunderstandings due to the lack of tone, social cues and context. If a conversation via email is causing confusion or escalating tensions, switching to a phone call can help clarify intentions and resolve issues more effectively.

4. Lengthy Back-and-Forth:

Engaging in a prolonged back-and-forth exchange via email can be time-consuming and frustrating. If it takes more than 2 replies to answer a simple question, it would be better to hop on a phone call to discuss the matter and take care of all questions in one fell swoop. This way, you save yourself and your team members the trouble of sending each other 20 emails!

5. Need for Immediate Feedback:

In situations where immediate feedback or input is required for an important project or meeting, a phone call would help to contact specific people more quickly in order to get the answer or approval you seek. For example, if you are preparing to meet with your supervisor in an hour and you are not clear on how to explain an issue, you could call up a fellow team member to brainstorm. By following this strategy, you won't have to stare at your inbox, anxiously waiting for someone to reply back to your email when you're under a time crunch.

6. Emotional or Personal Discussions:

Email lacks the emotional depth and empathy that are essential for sensitive or personal discussions. When addressing emotional issues, offering support, or providing feedback that may be difficult to convey in writing, a phone call allows for a more compassionate and empathetic exchange. You will have the space to actively listen, be heard, and express encouragement openly, in the way you intended.

7. Building Rapport or Strengthening Relationships:

Phone conversations offer a more personal and human connection compared to emails, making them ideal for building rapport, fostering relationships, or addressing interpersonal conflicts. Hearing someone's voice and engaging in spontaneous conversation can help you and the other person to get to know each other in a deeper way.

8. Multiple Stakeholders or Complex Dynamics:

In scenarios involving multiple stakeholders or complex dynamics, such as group discussions, negotiations, or cross-functional collaboration, navigating multiple opinions and ideas through email can be chaotic and hard to follow. A phone call allows for everyone to have a conversation where they can listen and take turns speaking, which would help to get everyone on the same page.

9. Desire for Clarity:

Some conversations require voice-to-voice communication or detailed explanations that may be lost in written form. For discussions involving subtle nuances, tone of voice, or non-verbal cues, a phone call can create a conversation space where it is easier for everyone involved to get a better read on how someone is feeling about a particular matter and how to approach them going forward.

In conclusion, while email remains a valuable tool for communication in the workplace, there are situations where a phone conversation is more appropriate and effective. By recognizing the signs that indicate the need for a phone call, individuals can ensure clearer communication, effective troubleshooting, and stronger relationships with colleagues and stakeholders.

The Rise of Artificial Intelligence (A.I.)

Is it wise to enlist the help of A.I. to write your emails? While A.I. has helped businesses to increase efficiency, save time, and conserve capital, they are not a perfect solution when it comes to communication.

Let's take a closer look:

Pro: A.I. can create something out of something, even when you have writer's block!

One advantage of using A.I. for writing emails is its ability to generate content, even when you're experiencing writer's block. A.I. algorithms can analyze prompts and generate text based on predefined patterns and data, providing a starting point for email drafts when inspiration is lacking. Whenever you have no idea how to write an email, you can always use A.I. to give you a boost.

Con: But you won't be able to copy-paste-and-send it before reading it first.

Despite its ability to generate text, AI-generated content often requires human intervention to sound natural and authentic. Therefore, you will usually need to look everything over to make sure it sounds like you, a real human being. While AI can provide a foundation for email drafts, you will need to make revisions to make it sound like something you would actually say in a conversation!

Pro: A.I. can use the same tone consistently across different emails and projects.

A.I.-powered email writing tools can help maintain consistency in tone, style, and branding across multiple emails. This is handy if you need to write a series of emails when time is limited. By analyzing patterns in language and content, A.I. algorithms can suggest phrasing and formatting choices that align with the organization's communication guidelines and objectives.

Con: However, the writing tone can be hit or miss.

Despite efforts to ensure consistency, the tone generated by A.I.'s may sometimes miss the mark or fail to capture your voice. Factors such as context, audience, and cultural references can influence how A.I. interprets and generates language, which may not line up with the message you are trying to get across.

Pro: Using A.I. can save you time by generating content instantly.

Using A.I. can significantly reduce the time and effort required to draft emails. When you give it a prompt, A.I. can create your full-length email in a matter of seconds. By getting more time back into your schedule, you will be able to focus more on higher-level tasks and priorities that need your attention.

Con: With A.I., you will need to experiment with different prompts to get the best email you can get.

While A.I. can generate content quickly, you may need to give it a few tries before settling on an email that best fits your needs. A.I. algorithms can only do as well as the information you give it. If you give the A.I. brief and vague prompts, you may get a less-than-desired result. However, if you are able to be very specific with your request and give it more information, then you will more likely generate an email that will make you happy.

Pro: Need help with brainstorming subject lines and greetings? A.I. can help with that!

If you're looking for subject lines, greetings, and other elements of email communication to grab your recipient's attention, A.I. is an amazing resource to help you brainstorm ideas. You can ask it to give you a list of potential options and once it has completed its task, all you need to do is look through and pick one you like.

Con: Make sure you pick wisely.

If you choose an idea generated by an A.I., make sure you stand by your choice because ultimately, you will bear the responsibility of presenting it to your team. At best, whatever ideas you are given by A.I., are starting points. It is up to you to use your sound judgment and discernment to figure out what idea is best for your current email communication.

What should you do?

Just remember, A.I. was created to be a tool to help you do your job faster and more efficiently. It's not meant to be something you can delegate to or take over a task completely. A.I. is a car and you are the driver. As long as you understand the limitations of A.I. and you arc willing to experiment to see how it can help you, go for it! Just be sure to read it over before hitting "send."

Email Do's and Don'ts

Now that you have a better understanding of how to master the art of email communication to navigate professional and personal interactions effectively in the fast-paced digital landscape, we're going to take things a step further. Together, we are going to delve into the fundamental do's and don'ts that can make or break your email exchanges. Read through each list carefully to get a better sense of how to better organize your emails, manage conflict with written communication, and how to properly address your clients, coworkers and boss through this media.

Formatting, Grammar, and General Etiquette

In the digital age, where communication often unfolds at the speed of light, the importance of formatting, grammar, and etiquette in email communication cannot be overstated.

Think of them as the pillars supporting the architecture of effective correspondence. Proper formatting ensures that your message is not only visually appealing but also easily digestible, guiding the reader's eye through your thoughts with clarity and precision. Grammar serves as the backbone of your message, providing structure and coherence that prevent misunderstandings and misinterpretations. Meanwhile, etiquette acts as the glue that binds it all together, fostering professionalism, respect, and rapport in your interactions. Together, these elements form the cornerstone of successful email communication, enabling you to convey your ideas with impact, integrity, and influence.

Don't: Write an email without considering WHY you're writing and who will be reading it.

Sending emails without considering their purpose and intended audience can lead to confusion and miscommunication. It's important to pause and think about why you're writing the email and who will be reading it to ensure that your message is clear, relevant, and appropriate for the recipient.

Do: Consider your messaging and your target audience.

Before composing your email, take a moment to consider the purpose of your message and the expectations and preferences of your target audience. Tailor your messaging to effectively communicate your intended message to the recipient, taking into account their perspective and needs.

Don't: Neglect to take the time to organize your email.

Disorganized emails can be difficult to read and may cause important information to be overlooked. Failing to organize your email properly can result in confusion and frustration for the recipient, hindering effective communication.

Do: Re-organize and reformat your email so it is not overwhelming.

Take the time to organize your email in a clear and logical manner, breaking down complex information into smaller sections or bullet points. Use formatting tools such as headings, paragraphs, and bullet points to structure your email effectively and make it easier to read and understand.

Don't: Write an email like it is a text message, like it's a dialogue sent one sentence at a time.

Email communication should be more formal and structured than casual text messaging. Sending emails with fragmented sentences or incomplete thoughts can be confusing and unprofessional.

Do: Write an email with appropriate background context and one or two focused questions.

Provide sufficient background information in your email to give context to your message and help the recipient understand its purpose. Focus on one or two main points or questions to keep your email concise and easy to follow.

Don't: Excessively use emojis in a business setting.

While emojis can add a touch of personality to your emails, excessive use of emojis in a business setting can come across as unprofessional and detract from the professionalism of your message. This may be a turn off for your customers and for your supervisor.

Do: Feel free to use one or two once in a while to make your email friendlier.

Use emojis sparingly to convey tone or emotion in your emails, but avoid overdoing it. Adding one or two appropriate emojis can help to soften the tone of your message and make it more engaging without detracting from its professionalism.

Don't: Pay no mind to the subject line.

Neglecting to create a clear and relevant subject line for your email can result in it being overlooked or ignored by the recipient. A vague or generic subject line may fail to convey the importance or urgency of your message.

Do: Make sure to make your subject lines relevant and specific.

Take the time to craft a descriptive and informative subject line that accurately summarizes the content or purpose of your email. A well-written subject line helps the recipient understand the importance of your message and encourages them to open and read it promptly.

Don't: Write long-winded and wordy emails.

Lengthy emails can overwhelm the recipient and make it difficult for them to extract the key information. Rambling or overly verbose emails may be disregarded or skimmed over, leading to misunderstandings or missed opportunities.

Do: Keep your emails short and concise.

Aim to communicate your message clearly and succinctly in your emails, focusing on the most important points. Be mindful of the recipient's time and attention span, and strive to convey your message efficiently without unnecessary elaboration.

Don't: Write big paragraphs.

Dense paragraphs can be intimidating to read and may discourage the recipient from engaging with your email. Large blocks of text can make it challenging to identify key information and follow the flow of your message.

Do: Use bullet points as much as possible and use smaller paragraphs

Break up large blocks of text into shorter paragraphs or bullet points to make your email more visually appealing and easier to digest. Using bullet points helps to organize your thoughts and highlights important information, making it more accessible to the recipient. If you have to make more than 2 points, list them with bullet points. For paragraphs, make them no longer than 4 sentences max.

Don't: Send an email full of grammar mistakes and typos.

Emails riddled with grammar mistakes and typos can undermine your professionalism and credibility. Poorly written emails may be perceived as careless or unprofessional, damaging your reputation in the eyes of the recipient.

Do: Read your email over and use Grammarly when needed.

Before sending your email, take the time to proofread it carefully for grammar, spelling, and punctuation errors. Consider using proofreading tools such as Grammarly to help catch any mistakes that may have been overlooked. Sending error-free emails demonstrates attention to detail and professionalism.

Don't: "Reply all" mindlessly.

Blindly hitting "Reply All" without considering whether all recipients need to be included in your response can lead to unnecessary email clutter and may inadvertently share sensitive information with unintended recipients.

Do: Double-check who your recipients are.

Before sending your reply, review the list of recipients to ensure that everyone included needs to receive your response. Consider whether "Reply All" is necessary or if your message can be directed solely to the relevant parties. Being mindful of who you include in your email communication helps prevent unnecessary email overload and maintains confidentiality when needed.

Don't: Ignore proper email etiquette.

Neglecting basic email etiquette guidelines can reflect poorly on your professionalism and may hinder effective communication with coworkers. It's important to avoid common email etiquette mistakes such as neglecting to use a subject line, sending emails with spelling or grammatical errors, or neglecting to include a proper salutation and closing.

Do: Follow established email etiquette guidelines.

Adhere to established email etiquette guidelines when communicating with coworkers to ensure professionalism and clarity in your messages. This includes using clear and concise language, proofreading your emails for errors before sending, and following proper formatting and structure.

Don't: Use email as the sole means of communication for urgent matters.

Relying solely on email for urgent matters can lead to delays in response times and miscommunication. If you are trying to correct something for a client and there is a large amount of money or risk involved, you will definitely need to make sure you address the matter quickly and get all hands on deck. For that reason, email may not be the most efficient or reliable method of communication for time-sensitive issues that require immediate attention.

Do: Use alternative communication channels for urgent matters.

If you need to communicate urgent information to a coworker, consider using alternative communication channels such as phone calls or instant messaging. Direct communication methods allow for real-time interaction and can help ensure that urgent matters are addressed promptly and effectively.

Don't: Use email as a platform for personal or sensitive discussions.

Discussing personal or sensitive matters via email can compromise privacy and may not be the most appropriate or secure communication method. It's important to avoid using email as a platform for discussing confidential information or sensitive topics that are better suited for face-to-face or private discussions. For instance, if you are speaking with the team member who is in charge of payroll, it is best to not send sensitive information such as social security or bank account numbers through email. Or if there is a personnel issue, email is not ideal.

Do: Use discretion and consider alternative communication methods for sensitive discussions.

Exercise discretion when discussing sensitive topics with coworkers and consider using alternative communication methods such as in-person meetings or secure messaging platforms for confidential or personal discussions. Choosing the appropriate communication method helps maintain privacy and ensures that sensitive information is handled appropriately.

Managing Conflict

In the realm of email communication, managing conflict is not just a skill—it's a crucial art form.

Conflict, whether born of differing perspectives, misunderstandings, or miscommunications, is an inevitable part of human interaction. However, in the digital arena, where tone and nuance can be easily lost in translation, the stakes of conflict resolution are even higher. Successfully navigating conflict within email communication requires finesse, empathy, and strategic diplomacy. It's about more than just addressing disagreements; it's about fostering understanding, building trust, and preserving relationships in the face of adversity. By approaching conflict with patience, active listening, and a willingness to find common ground, we transform email exchanges from battlegrounds into bridges, paving the way for resolution, growth, and strengthened connections.

Don't: Don't fire back at the other party until you have all the facts.

Reacting impulsively in the heat of a conflict can escalate tensions and lead to further misunderstandings. It's important to refrain from immediately responding with a defensive or confrontational tone until you have gathered all the relevant information and fully understand the situation from both perspectives.

Do: Cool off, collect your thoughts and look over your notes before engaging

Take the time to get your emotions in check and carefully review and compare your own understanding of the situation. By comparing notes and seeking clarification on any discrepancies or misunderstandings, you can gain a more comprehensive understanding of the conflict and identify potential areas of resolution or compromise. This approach promotes constructive dialogue and facilitates a more thoughtful and effective response that addresses the underlying issues.

Don't: Neglect taking notes or documenting important details

Failing to take notes or document key details during a conflict can lead to misunderstandings, discrepancies, and challenges in resolving the issue effectively. Without proper documentation, it becomes difficult to recall specific conversations, agreements, or actions taken, which may result in confusion or disputes later on.

Do: Document everything in writing as much as possible

Make it a priority to document all relevant information, discussions, decisions, and agreements related to the conflict in writing. Keeping detailed records allows for clarity, accountability, and reference points throughout the conflict resolution process. Written documentation provides a reliable reference for all parties involved and helps ensure consistency and transparency in communication and decision-making. By documenting everything in writing, you create a solid foundation for addressing the conflict and moving towards resolution effectively.

Don't: Engage in personal attacks or blame.

Resorting to personal attacks or assigning blame in email communication can intensify conflict and damage relationships. As tempting as it may seem in the moment, taking aggressive jabs at your recipient can actually make the situation worse, not better. It's important to avoid using accusatory language or making derogatory remarks that may escalate tensions and hinder resolution.

Do: Focus on the issue and express your perspective respectfully.

Keep the discussion focused on the specific issue at hand and express your perspective in a respectful and constructive manner. Use "I" statements to communicate how the conflict has impacted you personally and avoid placing blame on others.

Don't: Assume the other party's intentions or motives.

Jumping to conclusions about the other party's intentions or motives without sufficient evidence can lead to misunderstandings and further conflict. It's essential to avoid making assumptions and instead seek clarification to better understand their perspective.

Do: Practice high-level listening to seek understanding.

Listen attentively to the other party's viewpoint and seek to understand their concerns and motivations. Ask clarifying questions to gain insight into their perspective and demonstrate empathy and respect for their position.

Don't: Use email as the primary means for conflict resolution.

Relying solely on email to address conflict may limit effective communication and resolution. Email lacks the nuances of face-to-face interaction, making it challenging to convey tone and emotions accurately and resolve complex issues comprehensively.

Do: Consider alternative methods of communication or mediation.

If the conflict remains unresolved through email communication, consider alternative methods such as face-to-face meetings, phone calls, or mediation facilitated by a neutral third party. These methods allow for more direct and nuanced communication, facilitating greater understanding and resolution.

Don't: Engage in gossip and spread rumors.

Participating in gossip or spreading rumors via email communication can escalate conflict and damage trust among team members. Gossiping about others behind their back can create a toxic work environment and undermine morale. It's important to refrain from engaging in such behavior and instead focus on addressing conflicts directly and constructively.

Do: Set a good example.

As a leader or team member, setting a positive example for conflict resolution is essential in fostering a healthy work environment. Demonstrate integrity, professionalism, and respect in your email communication, even in the face of conflict. By modeling positive behavior, you encourage others to follow suit and contribute to a culture of open communication and mutual respect.

Writing To Clients

Every email sent to a client is an opportunity to convey professionalism, build trust, and strengthen rapport.

Clear and concise communication not only ensures that clients understand the information you're conveying but also demonstrates respect for their time and attention. Additionally, personalized and thoughtful emails show clients that they are valued and appreciated, fostering loyalty and long-term partnerships. Through effective email communication, you can manage expectations, address concerns, and provide timely updates, thereby enhancing transparency and accountability. Whether you're discussing project details, delivering reports, or simply checking in, each email serves as a reflection of your commitment to delivering exceptional service and exceeding client expectations.

Don't: Misrepresent your company when speaking with clients.

It's essential to maintain integrity and honesty in all interactions with clients. Misrepresenting your company's values, products, or services can erode trust and damage relationships with customers.

For instance, if your company is all about nurturing and encouraging your customers in a positive environment, using a voice and tone that suggests "tough love" and "suck it up" won't do. You have to maintain your integrity and protect the reputation of the company. Make sure your approach matches what your boss and your coworker would follow.

Do: Communicate consistently according to your company's brand values and voice.

Ensure that your communication aligns with the established brand identity and values of your company. Consistency in messaging helps reinforce the brand image and builds trust with customers. Your customers signed up because they expected to have a good experience with the company. The more you base your communication on your company's brand values and voice, the easier time you will have to give the experience the customer desires.

Don't: Send a reactive response to an upset customer.

Reacting impulsively to an upset customer can escalate the situation and lead to further dissatisfaction. It's important to avoid responding in haste without considering the best approach to address the customer's concerns. You may end up with an even bigger mess to clean up!

Do: Instead, send a proactive response.

Take the initiative to address the customer's concerns promptly and proactively. By acknowledging their issue and offering a solution or assistance before they escalate their complaint, you demonstrate commitment to customer satisfaction and can often prevent further dissatisfaction. Drive the solution forward and don't stress out about the problem.

Don't: Give your customer too much information to explain something to them.

Providing excessive or unnecessary information can overwhelm the customer and make it difficult for them to grasp the key points. It's important to avoid overwhelming customers with unnecessary details that may confuse or distract them from the main message.

Plus, you may risk giving away information that may be irrelevant to the situation and may make your customers question the competency of your abilities and your company's. For instance, if a glitch in the system artificially raises a customer's fee and they ask you about it, you don't need to describe every detail about the technical glitch. Instead, acknowledge a mistake was made due to a technical error and let the customer know exactly what you are going to do to fix this.

Do: Stay straight-to-the-point to give them an answer that satisfies their needs and protects the company.

Provide clear and concise answers that address the customer's inquiry or concern directly. By focusing on relevant information and avoiding unnecessary elaboration, you can effectively communicate the necessary information while respecting the customer's time and attention as well as yours.

Don't: Use inappropriate language, which could be offensive to someone's race, religion, ethnicity, health, age, economic status, appearance, and disabilities.

Using language that is offensive or discriminatory towards individuals or groups is unacceptable and can cause harm to the client, and damage yours and your company's reputation. It's important to avoid language that could be interpreted as disrespectful or discriminatory in any form of communication. Always put yourself in other people's shoes and walk a mile in them.

Do: Be Professional and Respectful.

Maintain professionalism and respect in all communications with customers, regardless of the circumstances. Even though you can't see their faces, please remember there is a whole human being on the other side. Treat customers with dignity and courtesy, using language that is appropriate and considerate of their backgrounds and sensitivities.

Don't: Come up with an answer from thin air for a situation you're not familiar with.

Providing inaccurate or uninformed responses can undermine trust and credibility with customers. It's important to avoid making assumptions or guesses when addressing unfamiliar situations or topics.

Do: Ask for help.

Seek assistance or guidance from colleagues or supervisors when faced with unfamiliar or challenging situations. If there is a company handbook full of policies, please make sure to review that if possible. By consulting with others who may have more knowledge or expertise, you can ensure that you provide accurate and helpful responses to customers.

Don't: Ghost a customer, even if you get busy.

Ignoring or neglecting customer inquiries or requests can lead to frustration, dissatisfaction, and complaints. It's important to avoid leaving customers waiting for a response or feeling ignored, even during busy periods.

Do: Find an organizational system that will allow you to keep all emails front and center.

Implement an effective organizational system to manage and prioritize customer emails, ensuring that no inquiries or requests are overlooked or forgotten. By staying organized and responsive, you can maintain positive relationships with customers and address their needs in a timely manner. If your company has a rule for responding back to customers within a certain time period, go by that policy. If your company does not have such a policy, a good rule of thumb is responding back within 2 business days or less.

Don't: Bend over backwards for your customers.

While it's important to provide excellent customer service, it's equally important to establish boundaries and maintain a balance between meeting customer needs and protecting the interests of the company. Going to excessive lengths to accommodate every customer demand can be unsustainable and may not align with company policies or objectives. You may end up spending a ton of time pleasing a customer for a task you're unable to fulfill or wasting your company's time and resources.

Do: Help out as best as you can, but set boundaries and follow the company's policies.

Strive to assist customers to the best of your ability within the framework of company policies and guidelines. While providing exceptional service is important, it's essential to set realistic boundaries and ensure that customer requests are managed in a way that aligns with the company's objectives and resources. For example, if a customer cancels their service and asks for a refund and your company has a "no refund" policy, you will have to uphold the company's policy but be empathetic to the customer. Here is an example, "Unfortunately, I can't give you a refund but I have paused your service so you will no longer be charged for anything else."

Don't: Ignore customer feedback, whether positive or negative.

Disregarding feedback from customers, whether it's praise or criticism, can lead to missed opportunities for improvement and relationship-building. Ignoring feedback or getting defensive may give the impression that their opinions are not valued, potentially resulting in decreased satisfaction and loyalty.

Do: Acknowledge and respond to all customer feedback.

Take the time to acknowledge and respond to customer feedback, expressing gratitude for positive comments and addressing concerns or complaints constructively. By demonstrating that you value their input and are committed to addressing their needs, you can foster trust and loyalty among customers.

Don't: Use generic or impersonal greetings.

Addressing customers with generic or impersonal greetings can create a sense of detachment and reduce the effectiveness of your communication. Customers appreciate personalized interactions that make them feel valued and respected as individuals.

Do: Use the customer's name and personalize your greetings.

Whenever possible, address customers by their name and tailor your greetings to reflect their unique identity. Personalized greetings demonstrate that you recognize and appreciate the individual behind the email, enhancing the customer experience and fostering a sense of connection.

Don't: Use jargon or technical language that customers may not understand.

Using overly technical language or industry jargon in customer communications can confuse or alienate customers who may not be familiar with such terminology. Clear and straightforward language is essential to ensure that customers understand the information being conveyed. Remember, the reason why your clients hired your company is because they are not the experts, and will therefore not understand all of the technical ins-and-outs.

Do: Use plain language and provide explanations when necessary.

Communicate with customers using language that is easy to understand and accessible to all. When using technical terms or industry-specific language, provide clear explanations to ensure that customers can follow along and grasp the key points of your message. Imagine speaking to a third grader. Keep it simple and basic.

Writing To Your Coworkers

Effective communication within a team is the lifeblood of collaboration, productivity, and cohesion.

When writing emails to coworkers and team members, the importance of clarity, transparency, and respect cannot be said enough. Being straightforward with your communication ensures that everyone is on the same page, minimizing misunderstandings and maximizing efficiency. In addition, upholding transparency establishes trust and creates a culture of openness and accountability within the team. By conveying information, updates, and expectations effectively, emails become more than just messages— they become catalysts for alignment, synergy, and collective success. Whether it's brainstorming ideas, delegating tasks, or providing feedback, every email exchange is an opportunity to strengthen bonds, leverage collective expertise, and propel the team towards its goals. Mastering the art of effective email communication among coworkers isn't just a nicety—it's a necessity for thriving in a collaborative environment.

Don't: Assume your coworker's availability or workload.

Making assumptions about your coworker's availability or workload can lead to miscommunication and frustration. It's important to avoid assuming that they are free to respond immediately or that they have the capacity to take on additional tasks without confirming with them first. Unless you are a mind reader, give them the benefit of the doubt.

Do: Respect your coworker's time and workload.

Before reaching out to a coworker via email, consider their schedule and workload. If you need their assistance or input, politely inquire about their availability and provide context for your request. Respecting their time and workload demonstrates consideration and professionalism. For non-urgent matters, give them two days to respond. If you still don't hear anything, send another email or call them. If a matter is urgent, call them on the phone to see if you can reach them. Should they not pick up, leave a voicemail indicating you need help with something right away and acknowledge that you would appreciate their help at their earliest convenience.

Don't: Use a demanding or confrontational tone.

Communicating with a demanding or confrontational tone can create tension, which can strain relationships with coworkers. When tension is high and conflicts come from and center, it is easy for things to get out of hand between you and your team members. Avoid using language that may come across as aggressive or disrespectful, as it can hinder effective collaboration and teamwork.

Do: Use a polite and respectful tone.

Maintain a courteous and professional tone in your emails to coworkers, regardless of the nature of your communication. Using polite language and showing respect for your coworker's perspective fosters a positive work environment and encourages open communication. If your coworker did something incorrectly, use this as a teaching moment to let them know what they did wrong and how to do better in the future.

Don't: Overload your coworker with unnecessary information.

Bombarding your coworker with excessive information can overwhelm them and make it difficult for them to focus on the key points of your message. It's important to avoid irrelevant details or tangents that may distract from the main purpose of your email.

Do: Provide clear and concise communication.

Keep your emails to coworkers clear and concise, focusing on the essential information they need to know. Use bullet points or numbered lists to organize complex information, and avoid including extraneous details that are not directly relevant to the subject at hand. If you get confused, think about why you are contacting your coworker about a particular issue and what kind of help you need from them.

Don't: Assume your coworker's familiarity with the topic.

Assuming that your coworker is already knowledgeable about the subject of your email can lead to misunderstandings or confusion. It's important to avoid making assumptions about their level of understanding and provide necessary context or background information to ensure clarity.

Do: Provide context and background information as needed.

When writing emails to coworkers, provide sufficient context and background information to help them understand the purpose and relevance of your message. Including relevant details or background context can facilitate effective communication and prevent misunderstandings. If your coworker has questions, be patient with them and answer them to the best of your ability.

Don't: Talk about personal matters excessively with your coworkers while you are clocked in, even if you are friends.

Engaging in excessive personal conversations during work hours, especially via email, can distract from job responsibilities and disrupt productivity. While it's natural to have friendly relationships with coworkers, it's important to maintain professionalism and focus on work-related tasks during work hours to ensure efficiency and effectiveness in the workplace.

Do: Take the time to get to know your coworkers to build a relationship with them and if there is mutual interest to be personal friends, hang out with them outside of work.

Building positive relationships with coworkers is important for collaboration and teamwork in the workplace. Taking the time to get to know your coworkers on a professional level fosters a supportive work environment and enhances communication and cooperation. If there is mutual interest in developing a personal friendship, it's appropriate to socialize outside of work hours to nurture those connections in a more relaxed setting, where you can discuss personal matters.

Writing To Your Boss

Writing emails to your boss doesn't have to be complicated, but you will still need to do your best to effectively communicate what's been going on with your projects and any updates having to do with your responsibilities.

Each email serves as a direct reflection of your professionalism, competence, and reliability. The more you can help your boss to understand your thoughts, requests, and updates without unnecessary confusion or ambiguity, the more you demonstrate your attention to detail and show respect for their time. These are essential qualities in any professional setting, especially when building trust and rapport with your boss. By putting extra attention to writing emails that are palatable and easy-to-understand for your boss, the more you invest into your future at the company.

Don't: Be overly casual or informal in your tone.

Maintaining a level of professionalism in your communication with your boss is essential. Avoid using overly casual language or slang that may be perceived as disrespectful or unprofessional. Don't focus on making your boss your friend. Instead, focus on treating your boss with respect and building a solid business relationship.

Do: Use a respectful and professional tone.

Address your boss with appropriate language and maintain a respectful tone throughout your email. Using formal language and proper etiquette demonstrates professionalism and respect for your boss's position. Your boss gave you the opportunity to work with them because they saw something in you. If they are treating you with respect, please reciprocate.

Don't: Ramble or include unnecessary details.

Your boss likely has a busy schedule and may not have time to read lengthy emails. If they are short on time and see that you sent them a super long email, they most likely won't read it and won't respond. Avoid overwhelming them with unnecessary information or lengthy explanations that could obscure the main point of your message.

Do: Be concise and to the point.

Get straight to the point in your email to your boss. Clearly state the purpose of your message and provide any necessary details concisely to ensure clarity and efficiency in communication. Have your most important points at the top of the email and use bullet points when necessary to organize the email and make it look less overwhelming.

Don't: Neglect to proofread your email.

Sending an email with spelling or grammatical errors reflects poorly on your attention to detail and professionalism. It's important to thoroughly proofread your email before sending it to your boss to avoid any mistakes. If your boss cannot understand what you are asking for in your email due to a series of typos, more time will be spent on clarifying your message rather than addressing the original issue head-on. Needless to say, grammatical errors can result in wasted time.

Do: Proofread your email for errors.

Take the time to review your email carefully for spelling, grammar, and punctuation errors before sending it to your boss. Double-checking your message ensures that it is polished and error-free, maintaining a professional image. Plus, your boss will have an easier time understanding why you reached out to them when they don't have to sort through misspellings or typos.

Don't: Make demands or be presumptuous.

Avoid coming across as demanding or presumptuous in your email to your boss. Making demands or assuming authority without proper justification can be perceived as disrespectful and may damage your professional relationship. Remember, your boss is human too! If you need to renegotiate something or give your boss feedback, always be professional first.

Do: Make polite requests and suggestions.

Frame your requests or suggestions in a polite and respectful manner. Use language that conveys appreciation for your boss's time and consideration, and provide rationale or justification for any requests or suggestions you make. Start by explaining what happened in a given situation, and then follow that up with "I recommend" in order to show that you are giving your boss a solution, not just complaining.

Don't: Disregard your boss's preferences or communication style.

Each person has their own communication preferences and style. Disregarding your boss's preferences or style can lead to misunderstandings and hinder effective communication. For instance, if your boss asks you to keep communication to email and only use text for urgent matters, please follow that request.

Do: Adapt to your boss's communication preferences.

Pay attention to your boss's preferred communication style and adjust your own communication accordingly. Whether they prefer brief and direct messages or detailed explanations, tailor your communication to meet their preferences for optimal understanding and collaboration.

Don't: Overpromise or exaggerate your accomplishments.

Exaggerating your achievements or making unrealistic promises in an email to your boss can erode trust and credibility. It's important to avoid overstating your accomplishments or capabilities, as it may lead to disappointment and undermine your professional reputation.

Do: Provide accurate and honest information.

Be honest and transparent in your email communication with your boss. Clearly communicate your achievements, progress, and any challenges you may be facing, providing realistic expectations and insights to facilitate effective decision-making and planning.

Don't: Avoid taking responsibility for mistakes or failures.

Shying away from accountability for mistakes or failures reflects poorly on your professionalism and integrity. Blaming others or deflecting responsibility in an email to your boss can damage trust and hinder your ability to learn and grow from setbacks. Admitting you made a mistake is scary, but it is always important to own what happened in order to maintain your integrity and get to a resolution faster.

Do: Take ownership of mistakes and failures.

Acknowledge any mistakes or failures openly and take responsibility for your actions in your email to your boss. Demonstrate accountability by outlining steps you plan to take to address the issue and prevent similar occurrences in the future, showing your commitment to learning and improvement.

Don't: Email sensitive or confidential information without proper precautions.

Sending sensitive or confidential information via email without proper security measures in place can pose a risk to privacy and confidentiality. It's important to avoid transmitting sensitive data in plain text without encryption or other protective measures. Some examples are social security numbers, banking information, customer credit card numbers, and passwords.

Do: Use secure methods for transmitting sensitive information.

If you need to share sensitive or confidential information with your boss via email, use encrypted email services or secure file-sharing platforms to protect the privacy and confidentiality of the data. If your workplace does not have a secure way to send sensitive information, call the recipient on the phone and give them the information that way. Taking precautions to safeguard sensitive information demonstrates profession-alism and respect for privacy.

Don't: Forget to express gratitude or appreciation.

Failing to express gratitude or appreciation in your email communication with your boss can come across as indifferent or ungrateful. It's important to acknowledge your boss's support, guidance, or feedback to maintain a positive and respectful relationship.

Do: Express gratitude and appreciation when appropriate.

Take the time to thank your boss for their support, feedback, or any assistance they have provided in your email communication. Showing appreciation demonstrates humility and fosters a culture of mutual respect and recognition in the workplace. You can never have too much gratitude, especially if it is from an authentic place!

Email Templates

Now that you have gotten this far into the book, let's put everything you learned into action!

Whether you need to look up examples to get a better idea on what you need to improve on with your email communication, or you need something to copy-and-paste to save you time, this is the section you've been looking for!

Study and save the email templates below, so you can find them whenever you need them.

Asking Your Coworker To Help Resolve An Issue, Version 1

Subject line 1: Need help, please!
Subject line 2: Issue with [Insert issue]
Subject line 3: Meeting request

Hi [Coworker's name],

Hope you are doing well!

I just heard back from [Insert informant's name] and found out there was an issue with [Insert issue] and now I need to figure out how to [Insert ideal solution].

I know you're busy, but would you be able to jump on the phone with me later today or early tomorrow to help me figure out [Insert specific information your coworker can help with]? I've already looked at [Insert first option], [Insert second option] and [Insert third option], but still can't figure it out.

Would appreciate any help you can give! Please let me know what your availability is.

Sincerely,
[Your Name]

Asking Your Coworker To Help Resolve An Issue, Version 2

Subject line 1: PLEASE READ ASAP!
Subject line 2: Please help!
Subject line 3: For immediate attention

Hi [Coworker's name],

Hope you are doing well!

I just heard back from [Insert informant's name] and found out there was an issue with [Insert issue]. Can you please [Pick one: pause/stop/reverse] [Insert what you need help with] immediately so we can fix this?

Thank you so much!

Sincerely,
[Your Name]

Reporting An Error or Mistake To Your Boss (Not resolved)

Subject line 1: Issue with [Blank]
Subject line 2: Please read ASAP
Subject line 3: My apologies!

Hi [Boss's name],

I regret to inform you that there is a problem with [Insert issue] due to [Insert cause of problem].

From what I understand, this is what happened:

- [FINDING 1]
- [FINDING 2]
- [FINDING 3]

My apologies for not catching this sooner. I'm working on getting this resolved immediately and will keep you posted.

If you would like to talk on the phone about this matter, please feel free to call me at your earliest convenience.

Sincerely,
[Your Name]

Reporting An Error or Mistake To Your Boss (Resolved) Version 1

Subject line 1: Resolved issue
Subject line 2: Please read ASAP
Subject line 3: Important heads up!

Hi [Boss's name],

Earlier today, I found out there was a problem with [Insert issue] due to [Insert cause of problem]. Because of this issue, [Insert secondary issue] occurred. Luckily, I was able to resolve the matter before [Insert other potential issue] occurred, thanks to [Insert resource or team member's name].

I apologize for the inconvenience this has caused.

To ensure this issue doesn't happen again, I am going to implement the following:

- [PREVENTATIVE MEASURE 1]
- [PREVENTATIVE MEASURE 2]
- [PREVENTATIVE MEASURE 3]

I believe all of these action steps will help to prevent this from happening again in the future.

If you would like to talk on the phone about this matter, please feel free to call me at your earliest convenience.

Sincerely,
[Your Name]

Reporting An Error or Mistake To Your Boss (Resolved) Version 2

Subject line 1: Resolved issue
Subject line 2: Problem with [Insert problem] [RESOLVED]
Subject line 3: Important heads up!

Hi [Boss's name],

Earlier today, I found out there was a problem with [Insert issue] due to [Insert cause of problem]. Because of this issue, [Insert secondary issue] occurred. Luckily, I was able to resolve the matter before [Insert other potential issue] occurred, thanks to [Insert resource or team member's name].

To ensure this issue doesn't happen again, here are my recommendations:

- [RECOMMENDATION 1]
- [RECOMMENDATION 2]
- [RECOMMENDATION 3]

I believe all of these action steps will help to prevent this from happening again in the future.

Please let me know if you have any questions or would like to meet to talk about everything in greater detail.

Sincerely,
[Your Name]

Reporting An Error To Your Client

Subject line 1: Notification: [Insert type of error] Error
Subject line 2: IMPORTANT ACCOUNT INFORMATION
Subject line 3: [URGENT] Important Account Information

Dear [Customer's name],

We regret to inform you that [Insert issue] has occurred, due to [Insert cause]. Your [Insert customer's property or information affected] was affected/breached and you currently won't be able to [Insert what they won't be able to do].

Rest assured, we are taking this matter very seriously and we are working hard to resolve this as quickly as possible.

If you have any questions, please reply back to this email or call us at [Insert phone number].

We will contact you as soon as everything is fixed.

We apologize for the inconvenience.

Sincerely,
[Your Name]

How to report findings that was requested by your boss or coworker

Subject line 1: Re: [Original subject line]
Subject line 2: My findings
Subject line 3: [Name of original request]

Hi [Boss or Coworker's Name],

I hope you are doing well!

As per your request, I looked into [Insert issue] and found out the following:

- [FINDING 1]
- [FINDING 2]
- [FINDING 3]

After looking at everything, I recommend we [Insert recommendation]. If you're not sure how to go about this, or if you have any other ideas, please let me know. I'd be happy to discuss this over the phone or in a meeting.

Please let me know if you have any questions.

Sincerely,
[Your Name]

Reminding a client to pay the invoice/sign the contract before starting the work

Subject line 1: [REMINDER] Please [Pick one or both: pay invoice/sign agreement]
Subject line 2: Checking in
Subject line 3: [PLEASE READ] Action required

Hi [Customer's Name],

How have you been?

I am writing to you today because I noticed you have not [Pick one or both: paid the invoice/signed the contract]. Please go ahead and do so at your earliest convenience in order to start the work.

If you have any questions, please do not hesitate to let me know.

Sincerely,
[Your Name]

Telling a client their fees will be increased

Subject line 1: Important Account Information
Subject line 2: [PLEASE READ] New Rates for [Insert year]
Subject line 3: Rate increase notification

Hi [Customer's Name],

We hope this email finds you well.

We are writing to inform you of an upcoming change that will affect your account. Due to various factors such as market conditions, inflation, and operational costs, we find it necessary to adjust our rates. Effective [Date of Rate Increase], we will be increasing your rate from [Insert old rate] to [Insert new rate].

We understand that any change in pricing may raise concerns, and we want to assure you that this decision was made after careful consideration. Our goal is to continue providing you with the highest quality service while ensuring that we can maintain the standards you expect from us.

We remain committed to transparency and open communication, and we want to be available to address any questions or concerns you may have regarding this rate adjustment. Please feel free to reach out to our customer service team at [Customer Service Number] or reply to this email, and we will be more than happy to assist you.

We greatly value your business and wanted to take a moment to express our gratitude for your continued support of our services.

Sincerely,
[Your Name]

How to respond to an unrealistic or out-of-scope request from a client

Subject line 1: Re: [Client's original subject line]
Subject line 2: Update on your request
Subject line 3: Update regarding your request

Dear [Client's Name],

I hope this email finds you well. I wanted to reach out to you regarding the recent request you submitted to us.

After careful review, we found that your request falls outside the scope of your current [Membership/package]. However, we understand the importance of this request to you and are committed to finding a solution that meets your needs.

Therefore, we're pleased to inform you that we can fulfill your request for an additional [Insert fee]. This will allow us to allocate the necessary resources and provide you with the service you require.

We value your business and want to ensure your satisfaction with our services. If you would like to proceed with the fulfillment of your request, please let us know.

Alternatively, if you have any questions or would like to discuss other options, please don't hesitate to reach out to us. We're here to assist you in any way we can.

Thank you for your understanding and cooperation. We look forward to continuing to serve you.

Best regards,
[Your Name]

How to give a suggestion to your coworker

Subject line 1: Thank you so much for your help!
Subject line 2: We make a great team
Subject line 3: A few ideas

Hi [Coworker's Name]

How is your [day of the week] going so far? Mine has been quite busy!

Thank you so much for all of your help with [Insert project]. We make a great team!

If you're up for it, I have a few ideas on how we can have an easier time tackling similar issues in the future. Please let me know if you would be interested to have a discussion.

Sincerely,
[Your Name]

How to give a suggestion to your boss

Subject line 1: Thank you so much!
Subject line 2: A few ideas
Subject line 3: Meeting request

Hi [Boss's Name],

How have you been?

Thank you so much for the opportunity to work on [Insert project]. It was so much fun and I learned a lot.

Now that everything has been completed, I had a few ideas that could improve how we go about similar projects. Would you be up for having a meeting so we can discuss?

Please let me know your thoughts.

Sincerely,
[Your Name]

Updating a Coworker/Boss the status of a project/service/request

Subject line 1: [Name of project/service/request] update
Subject line 2: Update on [Name of project/service/request]
Subject line 3: [Name of project/service/request] [Pick one: PROCESSING/IN PROGRESS/COMPLETE]

Hi [Coworker/s/Boss's name],

I hope you're having a fantastic [Insert day of the week].

Just wanted to leave a quick note to update you on the status of [Name of project/service/request].

The following items have been completed:

- [ITEM 1]
- [ITEM 2]
- [ITEM 3]

Here is what I have not completed, but will be working on over the course of [Insert time period]:

- [ITEM 1]
- [ITEM 2]
- [ITEM 3]

I'll give you another status update by [Insert date].

If you have any questions, please let me know!

Sincerely,
[Your Name]

Updating A Client On The Status of a Project/Service/Request

Subject line 1: [Name of project/service/request] update
Subject line 2: Update on [Name of project/service/request]
Subject line 3: [Name of project/service/request] [Pick one: PROCESSING/IN PROGRESS]

Hi [Client's name],

How have you been?

Just wanted to leave a quick note to update you on the status of [Name project/service/request]. Currently, [Name project/service/request] is [Pick one: processing/in progress] for the next [Insert number of days] days.

Once this is completed, we will move on to the next step, which is [Insert next step].

Please let me know if you have any questions. I would be happy to help!

Sincerely,
[Your Name]

Telling a Client a Project/Service/Request is Complete

Subject line 1: Your [Pick one: project/service/request] is complete!
Subject line 2: [Name of project/service/request] has been completed
Subject line 3: Your [Pick one: project/service/request] has been fulfilled

Dear [Client's Name],

Great news! Your [Pick one: project/service/request] has been completed!

It has been a pleasure to work with you. Thank you so much for your business and we look forward to working with you again in the future for all of your [Insert service] needs.

Please let me know if you have any questions or need anything else.

Sincerely,
[Your Name]

Telling a Coworker/Boss a Project/Service/ Request is Complete

Subject line 1: [Name of project/service/request] is DONE!
Subject line 2: [Pick one: project/service/request] status–
COMPLETED
Subject line 3: [Name of project/service/request] has been
completed

Hi [Boss's/Coworker's Name],

I'm happy to report that [Name of project/service/request] is
done! We are all set. Thank you so much for your patience
and flexibility.

Please let me know if you need anything else.

Sincerely,
[Your Name]

Confirming receipt to a client

Subject line 1: [Insert item received] received
Subject line 2: [Pick one: payment/signed contract/meeting request] receipt
Subject line 3: You are all set!

Hi [Client's Name],

Just wanted to drop a quick note.

We have received your [Pick one: payment/signed contract/meeting request] and it has been processed.

Now that everything has been settled, we will begin the work. We will send you the first draft within [Number] days.

Thank you so much for your business.

Sincerely,
[Your Name]

Checking in with a client when they haven't responded back in several days

Subject line 1: Checking in!
Subject line 2: Re: [Insert subject line of your last email]
Subject line 3: Are you okay, [Client's name]?

Hi [Client's Name],

How are you doing?

We haven't received a response from you since we sent our last message [Number] days ago and we are unable to move forward with [Name of project/service/request] without your input. Is there anything I can do to assist you?

Please let me know.

Sincerely,
[Your Name]

10 Bonus A.I. Prompts for Email Writing

Want to use A.I. to help you write emails when you just can't find the right words? Here are 10 A.I. prompts to copy-and-paste into your favorite A.I. software to save you time, energy and headaches. Use these as a helping hand when you are seeking to clarify your messages, enhance your professional tone, or simply boost your productivity.

Have fun!

Asking for help

Write an email to my [Pick one: Coworker/Boss], [Coworker's/Boss's name], to let him/her know I am having trouble with [Insert problem]. I know [he/she] is busy but I need [his/her] help.

Assistance with customer request

I need assistance with helping a customer with their request. Write an email to notify my [Pick one: team member/coworker] in the [Name of department], [Team Member's/Coworker's name], that I got a client request to [Insert change request]. The client's name is [Client's name]. This is important because [Reason why making this change is important to the company and to the client] if we don't complete this by [Deadline date]. I know he/she is busy and I really appreciate his/her help to get this done as soon as we can.

Change tone

I need to adjust the tone of my email. Take the following email and adjust the tone to be more [Insert adjective] and [Insert 2nd adjective], while maintaining professionalism. Integrate words such as [Insert preferred word] and [Insert 2nd preferred word]: [Copy and paste your original email here and then run A.I.]

Event announcement

Write an email announcing a work-related event to my coworkers. The event is called [Name of work event] and it is a [Type of event]. It will be held on [Event date] from [Start Time] to [End Time] at [Event location]. There will be [List what they can expect to see at the event]. Please RSVP to me by [RSVP cut-off date]. [Insert how many guests they can bring with them, if they are allowed to]

Internal meeting request to prepare for important presentation

Create an email to request a meeting with my [Pick one: Coworker or Boss], [Coworker's/Boss's name], to work on the presentation for the important meeting with our potential client, [Prospective client's name or company], in [Number] days. Ask them if they are available today or tomorrow for a phone call that should last only [Number] minutes. Make sure to let them know I appreciate their help.

Lengthen an email

Write a full-length email to my [Pick one: Coworker/Boss/Client], [Coworker's/Boss's/Client's name], with the following information: [List up to 5 updates]

Notifying a client of important changes

Write an email to our client, [Client's Name], to let her know we have made changes to [Insert what has been changed]. When he/she originally signed up, [Insert how things were previously]. Now, we will [Insert how things will change]. As of [Insert date], the new changes will take effect. [Insert how this will affect his/her and whether or not he/she needs to take any action]. The reason for these changes is [Insert reason for change].

Shorten an email

My email is too long. Please write a shorter version of this one, and use when necessary: [Copy and paste your original email here and then run A.I.]

Stop services to a client for unpaid invoices

Generate an email to send to a client, [Client's name], who has not paid his/her invoices after we reached out to them by email and by phone. If we do not hear back from her by [Date], we will effectively stop all [Type of services]. Please get in touch with us ASAP in order to avoid any interruption to your [Type of services].

Updating your boss on the status of a project

Create an email to send to my boss to update him/her on the status of the [Name of project]. So far, I have completed the [Action step 1, Action step 2, and Action step 3]. Next, I plan to work with [Collaborator's name] with [Department name or vendor company name] to make sure everything is all set for [Name of project] so we can have everything completed by [Deadline date]. Please include bullet points when possible.

Moving Forward

As we come to the conclusion of this email communication bible, it's essential to reflect on the journey we've taken together.

From mastering the fundamentals of formatting, grammar, and etiquette to navigating the nuances of conflict resolution and client communication, we've explored the intricate tapestry of email communication with curiosity and determination. As you close these pages, remember that communication is not just about words on a screen—it's about connection, understanding, and impact. Whether you're crafting emails for business, academia, or personal relationships, the principles and strategies shared in this book will continue to serve as your guiding light. May you always remember the importance of authenticity, empathy, and intentionality in every message you send.. Now, go forth and communicate boldly.

The world needs to hear your message.

About the Author

Amy Lanci is the CEO and Founder of Untold Story Enterprises. As a communication consultant, published author and professional speaker, she loves uncovering the gold within people and translating their dreams into words that resonate.

Born and raised in the Los Angeles County area of Southern California, Amy grew up as a second-generation Chinese American surrounded by her family and her melting pot of friends. Despite facing challenges such as speech delays and struggles with weight and emotional eating, Amy discovered her love for writing and marine biology in high school. After earning her undergraduate degree in Ecology, Behavior, and Evolution from the University of California, San Diego, she embarked on a career in sea turtle genetics. Her life changed when she received a diagnosis for non-alcoholic fatty liver disorder at the age of 24. This propelled Amy to confront her personal issues and embark on a path of healing and self-discovery.

Throughout her journey, Amy discovered what her gifts were and allowed herself to accept her voice by helping others to find power in theirs. Now, Amy is dedicated to empowering others to speak their truth and be heard. She has spoken on dozens of stages across the continental United States, presented at many online conferences, worked with clients from all around the world and published her first book in 2023, *Listen Up! The Secret Languages of Intuitives, Creatives and Analytical Thinkers.*

If you're struggling to articulate your message for your written or spoken communication, Amy would love to help!

Read more about Amy and her company at
https://untoldstoryenterprises.com

www.ingramcontent.com/pod-product-compliance
Lightning Source LLC
Chambersburg PA
CBHW070438130626
46553CB00006B/2246